ALL THINGS PENGUINS FOR KIDS

FILLED WITH PLENTY OF FACTS, PHOTOS, AND FUN TO LEARN ALL ABOUT PENGUINS

ANIMAL READS

THIS BOOK BELONGS TO...

_____

_____

WWW.ANIMALREADS.COM

CONTENTS

An Introduction to Penguins	1
What Is a Penguin?	7
Evolution of Penguins	21
Where Do Penguins Live?	27
Characteristics and Appearance	33
What do Penguins Eat?	47
Penguin Circle of Life	53
Awesome Facts!	57
Help Penguins Survive	67
Thank You!	71
References	73

AN INTRODUCTION TO PENGUINS

Penguins would have to be one of the most adorable animals in the world. Which other bird has flippers instead of wings, waddles on land but flies through water, and is always dressed up for a formal event?!

Keen to meet this adorable creature?

Then hold on tight, because we are going on a wonderful adventure to learn more about what makes penguins truly unique!

You probably already know that penguins are famous for being incredibly cute. They're also known for living on ice. Their funny waddle and plump bodies make it look like they'd trip over themselves any time. And they often do! This is why all penguins live in remote places that don't have land predators. If you've ever seen a penguin 'walk', then you'll know they would never be able to run away from a predator very fast!

In most pictures of penguins, you'll see them in big groups living on ice, although, to be honest, that is not the *only* place they live. There are many different species of penguins in the world, and not all like cold and icy landscapes – some prefer warmer seas and live close to the equator and even in Africa.

Penguins are such fascinating creatures — and not just because they look like they're wearing tuxedos! What makes them really interesting is that while they can't fly, they're fantastic swimmers. You can even say that if they joined the Olympics, penguins could easily beat humans in a swimming competition. This is because penguins can swim as fast as 15 miles per hour.

Do you know anyone who can swim that fast?

Penguins are also highly intelligent. Scientists who have studied them discovered that penguins can find the same nesting spot they've chosen every year. They also have a great sense of direction that keeps them from getting lost. With their knowledge of the environment, it's as if penguins have a built-in GPS or map in their brains.

One other thing that makes this creature clever is that they hunt in packs. This gives them a better chance of protecting themselves against predators in the water. At the same time, they can catch more fish if they hunt in groups.

You might think that penguins look like they're ready to party since they're dressed for one —

and you're not exactly wrong there. But you will soon learn that there is a very clever reason penguins look the way they do.

Penguins are very social animals, meaning they can communicate with other penguins and make friends with them. Because of this, they can tackle problems as a group. When fishing, penguins can even tell other penguins where the fish are by signaling to the flock!

There are many other things that make studying penguins worthwhile.

If you're ready to know more about them, keep reading and discover the delightful world of penguins!

WHAT DO PENGUINS WEAR IN THE SUMMER?

Flipper Flops!

WHAT IS A PENGUIN?

If you want to know more about penguins, it's best to start with what they are.

Many people think penguins are mammals (like us humans, dogs, cats, and monkeys, and even whales), but this is not true. You may be surprised to know that penguins are actually birds.

Unlike other birds, however, penguins can't fly, and this is probably why people think they're mammals. Have you ever seen a penguin fly? No?! Exactly! Most photos of penguins show them on land, although this is another misunderstanding.

In truth, penguins spend around 80% of their lives in the water. Can you imagine spending a good part of your day on the beach or in the pool? Yes, we agree, that would be pretty cool, although our skin would get all wrinkly, given we are mammals who belong on land. Penguins, however, are more like sea birds instead of the usual flying birds.

On land, penguins can look quite clumsy, but they're graceful and efficient swimmers underwater.

Penguins have big families. Their colonies can reach from a few hundred to several thousand, and even a million! In some places, there are more penguins than there are people.

Right now, there are about 18 species of penguins known to humans. They can be divided into 6 groups based on what they look like. These 6 groups are the Crested group, the Banded group, the Brush-Tailed group, the Large group, the Yellow-Eyed group, and the Little or Fairy penguins.

It would take a pretty long time if we name all the penguins, so here are some examples of penguins belonging to each of the 6 groups:

A Macaroni Penguin, *Photograph by: kuhnmi - Creative Commons License*

MACARONI PENGUINS

Macaroni penguins belong to the Crested group. They're called "crested" because they have a crown of yellow feathers on their head, which are called crests.

Despite their funny name, Macaroni penguins don't look like pasta. Sorry to disappoint, but they don't eat mac and cheese, either. Macaroni penguins got their name from the feathers of a giant hat that was very popular 300 years ago. Macaroni hats have feathers that resemble the yellow feathers on top of a Macaroni penguin's head.

Aside from having a peculiar name, Macaroni penguins are the most populous species. They can live for about 8 to 15 years (which is actually a very long time in bird years), can grow to around 27.5 inches in height (about as tall as a big bike wheel), and can weigh between 8 and 14 pounds. This makes them just a bit lighter than a TV!

Two African penguins waddling on the beach.

AFRICAN PENGUINS

African penguins belong to the Banded group. They live on the southern shores of Africa and are the only penguin species that live on that continent. They have a black band of feathers on their white bellies, which is what makes them part of the Banded group. This black band comes in the shape of an upside-down horseshoe.

African penguins can be *really* noisy, and some say their sounds resemble the shrill braying of a donkey. If you've ever heard what a donkey sounds like, that's what African penguins sound like, too. Their colonies can also be large, so you can just imagine how loud they can be!

So how can penguins cope with the hot weather in Africa, you ask? Well, they have developed very unique glands just above their eyes. When it gets too hot, the glands expand, allowing their blood to cool down. How neat is that?!

African penguins may be loud, but they are pretty small. They can weigh between 5 and 9 pounds and grow between 23 inches and 25 inches tall. That's about the same as stacking two of your school rulers on top of each other.

Two Gentoo penguins taking a break from diving.

GENTOO PENGUINS

Gentoo penguins belong to the Brush-tailed group because, well, their tails look like brushes. Gentoo penguins are the largest of the bunch at 32 inches. They can also grow to be as heavy as 15 pounds. This makes them just a bit heavier than the biggest Macaroni penguins!

Gentoo penguins are the fastest swimmers among all the penguin species. They can swim four times faster than an Olympic swimmer, at a speed of 23 miles per hour! They can also make over 400 dives in just a single day – how crazy is that?!

| Emperor penguins on ice!

EMPEROR PENGUINS

Emperor penguins belong to the Large group because they're actually the largest of all the penguin species. They can grow as tall as 51 inches — maybe that's as tall as you!

At 88 pounds, Emperor penguins also weigh just a little more than you probably do.

Being giant-sized isn't the only thing that makes Emperor penguins unique. They're famous for being the Olympic divers of the bird world since they can dive down deeper than any other penguin.

Since they are so very big, Emperor penguins can also stand much colder temperatures than all the other penguins. They are the only species that live in Antarctica in winter.

Did you know this is the coldest, driest, and harshest continent on earth?! Well, the Emperor penguins are tough creatures indeed. So tough, in fact, that they incubate their eggs during the coldest, harshest and darkest days of winter.

And do you know what else? Emperor penguin moms lay only one egg at a time. Then, they place it between the dad's feet and he sits on this egg for two months to keep it warm and protect it from the very harsh elements. They don't move from their spot even if it gets extremely cold or the winds become unbearable!

Close up of a Yellow-eyed penguin.

YELLOW-EYED PENGUINS

Yellow-eyed penguins have a yellow mask over their eyes, like goggles, which is how they got their name. They can be really private penguins and don't like to have nosy neighbors. When another pair of penguins are nesting close to them, yellow-eyed penguins might choose to leave their nest. If you've ever had a really nosy neighbor, you might understand them a little better!

Yellow-eyed penguins can be as tall and heavy as their penguin cousins in Africa. They can also grow up to 25 inches and weigh up to 5 pounds, like half a carton of soda pop!

A tiny Fairy penguin laying down.

LITTLE PENGUINS OR FAIRY PENGUINS

Little penguins or Fairy penguins are the smallest of all the penguins. You can usually find them at the base of sandy dunes or cliffs. By the time they're 3 years old, fairy penguins are considered adults.

They're also lightweight and usually only weigh 2-3 pounds. That's half the weight of an average newborn human baby. Since they're also the tiniest of penguins, fairy penguins only grow up to about 12 inches tall. That's about the size of one school ruler.

Even though they're named fairy penguins, they don't carry around pixie dust. Because, hello? They don't even have pockets! But you can probably fit them in one — though it's best not to try.

What's your favorite penguin so far?

WHAT DO YOU CALL A COLD PENGUIN?

A Brrr-d!

EVOLUTION OF PENGUINS

According to scientists, penguins have been around for a really, really long time — about 60 million years, in fact. They're believed to have lived somewhere close to New Zealand in a place without land predators.

Since they didn't have to protect their nests by building them on trees like other birds do, penguins survived without ever needing to fly. So, over time, they simply forgot how to. Because they live near the water, they adapted to their environment and became excellent swimmers instead.

Penguins look a lot like another kind of bird: the puffins of the Northern Hemisphere. Puffins also have black and white bodies, so people easily confuse the two. But penguins and puffins are not exactly related.

A puffin eating a fish.

The great auk, a flightless bird that also looks like penguins, is not related to penguins either.

It's the puffins who are more like the cousins of great auks.

Great auks are extinct now, meaning you can't find one anywhere in the world. Whalers and fishers turned them into food and, eventually, the planet just ran out of them about 200 years ago.

Great auks were the first ones to be called penguins. Nobody knows for sure where the name came from, but some say it could have come from Welsh or Spanish words. In Welsh, the words "pen" and "gwyn" mean white head. In Spanish, the term "pingüino" describes how penguins have extra body fat.

When the great auks were gone, seafarers and explorers might have been surprised to see another type of bird that looked similar to them. It's how the penguins we know today are called penguins, even though they aren't related to great auks.

WHERE DO PENGUINS LIVE?

Many cartoons often show penguins living in the North Pole (the Arctic) or the South Pole (Antarctica), **but this is a myth.** Polar bears live in the Arctic, but that's a story for another time (and book)!

Some penguins live in Antarctica, a continent that is mostly covered in ice. Many people probably mistake this for the Arctic because this is also a region covered in ice, and the names kind of sound similar, right? Yet, in reality, only two species of penguins live in Antarctica: the Emperor and Adélie penguins. All the other species live in all sorts of places, although some visit Antarctica from time to time. Penguins who visit

Antarctica do so in the southern summer, where they stay for a few months to breed and lay eggs.

Antarctica, *Photograph by: Christopher Michel - Creative Commons License*

So, where exactly do penguins live?

You can find most penguins in the Southern Hemisphere. These include places like Australia, Africa, New Zealand, and many others.

Penguins live near bodies of water because that's where they get their food. While there's no ice, places near water usually have a cooler temperature. It's how penguins can survive even if there's no ice. Their feathers are insulating (like your winter jacket, if you live in a cold place!), and that's what helps survive the cold. Most penguins also have oil on their bodies and a good amount of body fat that keeps them warm.

Only one species of penguin lives in the Northern Hemisphere: the Galápagos penguin. They live on the Galápagos Islands, which is where their name comes from. The Galápagos Islands are volcanic islands found off the coast of Ecuador in the Pacific Ocean, and they are magical islands full of super interesting animals.

Penguins in the Galápagos Islands

Even though it can get hot in the Galápagos Islands, the Galápagos penguins are tiny, so they can crawl inside caves. This lets them avoid the heat on the land.

Have you traveled to any of these places? Have you seen the penguins there?

WHAT IS A PENGUIN'S FAVORITE FAMILY MEMBER?

Aunt Artica!

CHARACTERISTICS AND APPEARANCE

By now, you know that penguins can't fly and that they evolved flippers instead of wings, so they can glide easily at sea. Penguin flippers act just like boat paddles because they're stiff. The cool thing about them is that penguins can make their flippers rotate in different ways at the same time!

Unlike other birds, the bones that make up a penguin's "wings" aren't lightweight at all. Penguin flippers are made of solid bones that let them swim faster. It's because these bones are heavy that makes them unable to fly.

Many scientists believe that penguins became better swimmers because they lived closer to the water. Since they relied on the water for food, they had to learn how to swim fast, so they could catch food.

Over time, their bodies became better suited for swimming instead of flying.

Aside from being great swimmers, penguins are also excellent divers. They can dive hundreds of meters underwater when hunting for food. Some of the best penguin divers are the Emperor penguins, Gentoo penguins, and King penguins.

Parts of a Penguin

WALKING, WADDLING, AND WEBBED FEET

On land, penguins walk very slowly and take small steps. Their bodies sway from side to side, **which is called waddling**. Because of their walk, a group of penguins on land are actually called a waddle.

Even though they might look a little clumsy, penguins can actually walk up to 60 miles across the ice! That's pretty far for someone with tiny steps!

They can also slide across the ice using their bellies. Their feet are what push them forward. This is called "**tobogganing**."

A group of Emperor Penguins tobogganing and waddling across the ice.

Because of their speed and shape, penguins can look like fluffy torpedoes while tobogganing!

Wouldn't it be fun to do that?

When in the water, penguin feet can also be pretty amazing. That's because they're webbed and better as flippers. When swimming, penguins use their feet to steer in the water. Along with their flippers, penguin feet make them expert swimmers. They're actually so good at swimming that they can even look like they're "flying" in the water!

When a large group of penguins gather in the water, **they're called a raft**. A raft is also another word for a boat or floating machine made of logs or timber fastened together.

ARE PENGUINS REALLY WEARING TUXEDOS?

They might look like it, but penguins aren't actually wearing tuxedos. What they have are white underbellies and black backs. This can look a little funny sometimes since they're not really going to a formal party (*or are they?*)

But the way penguins look isn't just for show. It's actually nature's way of letting them hide from predators or hunt their prey. This funny but clever tuxedo look is called **countershading**.

What does this mean?

When you look at the ocean from above, the surface can look like it's dark blue or even black. Because of their black feathers, it's hard to spot a penguin from the surface of the water.

On the other hand, if you're swimming in the ocean and you look up, you'll see a really bright surface. This is because the sun is being reflected on the water. Thanks to their white underbellies, penguins are then also hard to spot underwater.

Yes, penguins may look like they're all dressed up for a fancy night out, but, as it turns out, they are simply camouflaged!

Every year, penguins shed their old black and white feathers. This is called molting. You can say that it's like changing their clothes. Eventually, these feathers grow back, making them look like they're wearing shiny new tuxedos.

Even if they don't have mirrors, penguins still spend a lot of time fixing their appearance. They oil, wash, and straighten out their feathers. It's the same as when we comb our hair or brush our teeth! Penguins just take a longer time to finish. This is called preening.

It's possible that penguins use the water to look at their reflections. But nobody really knows.

What do you think?

A penguin *preening*.

PENGUINS HAVE UNIQUE FEATURES, TOO!

Though all penguins can sometimes look the same, they have a few features that can separate them from others of their kind.

Most of the time, the names penguins are called by describe the features they're known for. Remember the Crested penguins? They're called this because their heads have a crown of yellow feathers. Of course, you already know that the Macaroni penguins don't look like pasta.

Other penguins have similar yellow feathers on them, but they look more like their eyebrows instead of their hair. Some penguins with bushy yellow eyebrows are the Fordland Royal, Rockhopper, and Snares.

Yellow-eyed penguins don't exactly have yellow eyes. Instead, they look like they're wearing a yellow mask over their eyes. Maybe it's to hide a secret superhero penguin identity!

Then there are the Emperor and King penguins. You might think they have crowns or long capes, but they don't, unfortunately. What they do have are orange and yellow marks on their necks. If you've ever watched the movie *Happy Feet*, Mumble is actually an Emperor penguin!

Speaking of *Happy Feet*, penguins can actually sing. It's what they use to attract their mates. This is because penguins have a unique voice. The lower the voice of a male penguin, the more attractive they are to females. If male penguins have a deep voice, this usually means they're big and fat. Females tend to choose the big, fat penguins because it means they can keep the eggs warm during breeding season.

Aside from attracting mates, the unique voice of a penguin can also be heard by their babies. It's how penguin chicks recognize their parents. This comes in handy when a penguin chick looks for its mom and dad after they've come back from hunting food.

Much like people, different penguins have different features.

Which penguin do you think is the cutest?

WHY WOULD PENGUINS CROSS THE ROAD TWICE?

To prove they aren't chicken!

WHAT DO PENGUINS EAT?

Penguins are carnivores. This means they only eat meat because they need a lot of protein and fat to keep themselves warm. Growing kids like you, though, still have to finish your greens!

Since they usually live next to the water, penguins eat fish, crustaceans (*sea creatures with shells*), and other marine life.

Bigger penguins can also eat squid or cuttlefish. These cephalopods (soft sea creatures with a head and lots of tentacles) are usually found deep underwater. Luckily, bigger penguins can dive hundreds of feet in the water. Some penguins can even go as deep as 900 feet!

Smaller penguins can't dive as deep, so they eat smaller fish or krill (tiny crustaceans). Small penguins can dive between 6 and 150 feet.

Penguin eating a fish, *Photograph by: dirrgang - Creative Commons License*

Even though they're meat-eaters, you'd be surprised to know that penguins don't have teeth. What they have instead are spines inside their beaks. They even have some on their tongue!

These spines can look like teeth, but they're not like our teeth at all.

A penguin's mouth and tongue spines point backward. These help them hold onto the fish or prey they've caught. It also helps them swallow.

Unlike other animals, penguins don't chew their food. They swallow it whole.

A penguin feeding its chicks.

Their gizzards (the muscles in their tummies!) break the food down. Some penguins can keep their food inside their stomach for days. A special chemical inside their body keeps the food from going bad.

When feeding their baby penguins or chicks, parent penguins digest the food first. Then, they bring the digested food back up to their beaks. The beaks of parent penguins act like a spoon. They would use this to place the digested food inside their chick's mouth. Yep, it sounds kinda gross, but hey, it's their eating habit!

Can you guess what a penguin's favorite food is?

WHY DO PENGUINS ALWAYS CARRY FISH IN THEIR BEAK?

Because they haven't got any pockets!

PENGUIN CIRCLE OF LIFE

The life cycle of penguins is pretty simple. You can summarize it in four stages:

- **Stage 1:** Egg
- **Stage 2:** Chick
- **Stage 3:** Young adult
- **Stage 4:** Adult

Unlike other birds that lay several eggs, penguins lay only one or two eggs at a time. But they do keep their eggs warm between their legs, which is what other birds also do. Penguin moms and dads take turns doing this. Except for the Emperor penguin eggs, as you know, that are warmed only by their dads. Emperor penguin moms go out for several weeks to hunt for food while dad is (literally) baby-sitting.

When the eggs are ready to hatch, the penguin chicks inside will use their beaks to break the shell. This can take as long as three days. When they've finally come out of the shell, penguin chicks will feel really hungry. Parents then take turns feeding them.

When the penguin chicks become a little older, their parents leave them behind to hunt for food. To keep themselves warm, the baby penguins huddle together while waiting for their parents to return. Penguin parents can tell which chicks are theirs through the sound of their voices.

When they finally reach adulthood, penguins will be ready to mate. During mating season, adult penguins will come ashore and find a mate. Most penguins breed during the spring and summer. Once they attract a partner, these adult penguins are ready to become parents.

AWESOME FACTS!

As you can see, penguins are fascinating creatures. Aside from the stuff we already mentioned, there are still a lot of astonishing facts about penguins! Here are more things you should know about these cute, flightless birds:

PENGUINS POOP A LOT

Yes, penguins poop *a lot*! It's because they have a speedy metabolism. This means they digest food quickly, so they need to go potty every 20 minutes.

Yet penguins don't have bathrooms, so they poop on the ground. Sounds yucky, right? It would be for you and me, but it's different for penguins. Just be warned: if you are ever lucky enough to visit a penguin colony, be ready to *smell* it before you even see it!

Because penguins' colonies can be very big, their homes can smell pretty bad, but this isn't such a terrible thing all the time. Thanks to the dark stains penguin poop leave on ice, scientists and researchers can keep track of them easily — even from space!

A Chinstrap Penguin relaxing on a rock.

Now, there's one species of penguin that's notorious for *flinging* poop: the Chinstrap penguins. They might not be so big, but they can have pretty bad tempers. When they're mad, they fling poop around and get into fights with other Chinstrap penguins.

PENGUINS CAN BE LIFETIME PARTNERS

Adult penguins can get married, though not in the same way humans do. Most of the time, penguins find one mate and stay with them for many years. Sometimes, they even stay together for life. This can be rare among animals, who often choose other partners when the next mating season comes.

Even among a crowd of hundreds or thousands of other penguins, one partner can find their mate by picking up the sound of their voice.

PENGUINS PROPOSE WITH STONES

Speaking of mating, male penguins have a strange but romantic way of proposing to their mate — they give them a pebble. It might be silly to us, but it makes sense to penguins since they don't have fingers for a wedding ring. Because duh!

Male penguins spend hours and hours searching for the perfect pebble for the love of their life. When they finally find this perfect little stone, they present it to their soon-to-be soulmate. If the female penguin accepts, then they can get "penguin married."

Nobody really knows how penguins throw wedding parties. People just assume they do because they're already dressed for the occasion!

PENGUINS ARE FEARLESS ON LAND

Penguins face a lot of predators in the water, like killer whales and leopard seals. On land, they don't face many threats from other animals. It's why they didn't evolve for flight in the first place.

Because penguins have spent millions of years living in places without land predators, they can be pretty fearless out of the water. Unlike other animals who can be scared of people, penguins might not run away when they see you. In fact, they might just get up close and personal. Penguins are known to be very curious animals!

PENGUINS HAVE AMAZING LUNGS

Remember how penguins can dive hundreds of meters underwater? It's not just their flippers or feet that let them do this really well. Penguins also have amazing lungs that can allow them to hold their breath for up to 20 minutes or more!

The longer penguins stay underwater, the deeper they can dive. The longest penguin dive recorded is around 28 minutes. How impressive!

PENGUINS CAN ADOPT

Believe it or not, penguins can also feel heartbroken, especially if their baby dies. When this happens, a mom penguin goes around the colony to look for abandoned penguin chicks. When they find one, they'll adopt this chick and raise it as their own. Sometimes, it's not only penguins they adopt but also other birds of other species.

SOME PENGUIN POPULATIONS OUTNUMBER PEOPLE

While some penguin species are endangered, like the Galápagos penguin, Yellow-Eyed penguin, and Northern Rockhopper, other penguin populations can be vast. In fact, the largest penguin population lives on South Sandwich Island – which is a curious name for a very dramatic island. Over two million penguins make up the colony there — what a large town!

A King Penguin Colony

EMPEROR PENGUINS LIVE TO THE EXTREME

You know now that penguins are excellent swimmers and great divers. But did you know that Emperor penguins can climb steep ice cliffs?

That's right! Emperor penguins have mighty feet that can let them climb these high ice cliffs without falling. They can also breed on ice shelves if they run out of sea ice.

HELP PENGUINS SURVIVE

*D*id *you enjoy learning about penguins?*

If you did, you should know one very important thing about them: some penguins are in danger of losing their habitat. Like many animals, penguins are also affected by climate change. One of the things that climate change does is make the oceans feel hotter. This melts the ice that penguins live in. It also affects their food supply and nutrients.

Luckily, there are many organizations that try to battle the effects of climate change on animals. Some of these are the World Wildlife Fund and the Wildlife Conservation Network.

Penguins can also be affected by what humans do. Aside from climate change, some of the challenges penguins face are commercial fishing or infectious diseases brought by humans. This is the reason that anyone visiting Antarctica on a big expedition ship is not allowed to set foot on land if they have a cold or a stomach bug! The risk of infecting the resident penguins would be too great.

Still, it's not too late to help penguins survive and keep their habitat. Caring for the environment is a little way to help penguins a lot.

Have you thought about what you can do to care for the environment?

THANK YOU!

Thank you for reading this book and for allowing us to share our love for penguins with you!

If you've enjoyed this book, please let us know by leaving a rating and a brief review wherever you made your purchase! This helps us spread the word to other readers! Thank you for your time, and have an awesome day!

For more information, and to find more great reads about awesome animals please visit:

www.animalreads.com/books/

© Copyright 2021 - All rights reserved Admore Publishing

ISBN: 978-3-96772-075-4

ISBN: 978-3-96772-076-1

ISBN: 978-3-96772-083-9

ISBN: 978-3-96772-084-6

Animal Reads at www.animalreads.com

The content contained within this book may not be reproduced, duplicated or transmitted without direct written permission from the author or the publisher.

Under no circumstances will any blame or legal responsibility be held against the publisher, or author, for any damages, reparation, or monetary loss due to the information contained within this book. Either directly or indirectly.

Cover Design by Krisssmy.

The Icons & images used in this work were from:

- Smashicons
- Flaticon
- Freepik

Published by Admore Publishing: Roßbachstraße, Berlin, Germany

www.admorepublishing.com

REFERENCES

Interested in learning more about penguins?

Check out some of these great resources online. Some of the information on these pages were even used to help create this book.

https://www.cabq.gov/artsculture/biopark/news/10-cool-facts-about-penguins

https://stacker.com/stories/3840/penguins-25-fascinating-facts-about-these-flightless-friends

https://www.nationalgeographic.com/animals/birds/facts/penguins-1

REFERENCES

https://www.treehugger.com/places-see-penguins-in-the-wild-4858671

https://sciencing.com/penguins-feed-their-chicks-4567587.html

https://www.wwf.org.uk/learn/fascinating-facts/emperor-penguins

https://www.treehugger.com/penguin-facts-5116139

https://seaworld.org/animals/all-about/penguins/habitat-and-distribution/

https://ocean.si.edu/ocean-life/seabirds/penguins

www.ingramcontent.com/pod-product-compliance
Lightning Source LLC
LaVergne TN
LVHW020135080526
838202LV00047B/3944